Spirit Voyage's

KUNDALINI TRANSFORMATION KIT

YOGA AND MANTRAS FOR PROSPERITY

BRING WEALTH AND ABUNDANCE INTO YOUR LIFE

by GURUGANESHA SINGH AND KARAN KHALSA

Printed in USA

ISBN-10: 0983569517
ISBN-13: 9780983569510

About the Kundalini Transformation Kit

SPIRIT VOYAGE has created the Kundalini Transformation Kit series to offer a set of meditations and principles to live by to support your life's needs. This tool kit incorporates Kundalini Yoga as taught by Yogi Bhajan®, whose powerful yogic technology supports so many aspects of our day-to-day lives.

It is our hope that using these tool kits will provide you with a source to improve your life and transform it into the manifestation of your hopes for your self and your soul.

Spirit Voyage believes that music has the power to transform the planet, one person at a time. By incorporating the beauty of the sound current into these yogic meditations, we use the technology of Naad yoga to create a vibration that imprints the impact of these meditations deep into the psyche.

You can use these meditations one by one, practicing each one for 11 to 40 days, or you can use them in combinations, practicing them at different times of day. Create a sacred space in your home to practice these meditations. Allow yourself to immerse yourself in the experience of them.

WE WISH YOU DEEP AND POSITIVE TRANSFORMATION!

CD Tracks

Music for Prosperity

1. Bountiful, Blissful, Beautiful
by GuruGanesha Singh and Snatam Kaur ~
Prosperity Affirmation

2. Prosperity Har by Prabhu Nam Kaur & Snatam Kaur ~
Powerful Prosperity Meditation

3. Bahota Karam by Sat Hari Singh and Hari Bhajan ~
Nanak's Abundant Gifts Meditation

4. Ardas Bhaee by Mirabai Ceiba ~
Meditation for Your Life's Needs

5. Har Har Har Har Gobinday by GuruGanesha Singh ~
Fearless Prosperity Meditation

Table of Contents

The Guiding Principles of Prosperity
by GuruGanesha Singh

THE GUIDING PRINCIPLES OF PROSPERITY CONSCIOUSNESS

By GuruGanesha Singh

To me, prosperity is a flow. I live my life doing things that keep me in the flow and avoiding things that block the flow. Playing music puts me in the flow, and I devote my life to that. Prosperity is a flow, not just from the Universe to you, but also from you to the Universe. Giving puts you into the flow and creates the opening for you to receive. For me, music is both. I receive so much from the Universe when I play music, and I know that I give back to the Universe through playing music. This is what we all need to find for ourselves, and prosperity will abound.

Prosperity consciousness is very much a state of mind. You must have trust in the flow. You must trust that if you give, you will receive. Then you can spend your life focusing on doing what fulfills you, knowing you will in turn be completely taken care of.

For a spiritual person, I recommend the entire focus be the prayer "Thy will be done. Dear Lord, how can I best serve?" Not on money. For the last 40 years, I have continuously prayed to my guardian angel and teacher, Guru Ram Das. Whatever has come before me, I put my full energy into excelling at it, even when it came to washing dishes in my first ashram in 1973. After two to three months of negativity, when I embraced the mantra and the teachings, I felt an overwhelming sense of gratitude.

I believe that in my life, I have been prosperous because I have zero fear that I'm not going to be provided for. It doesn't matter what your net worth is. If you believe everything is going to be provided for, you are a prosperous person. If you are in a state of fear that there's not going to be enough, that fear is the opposite of prosperity consciousness. Prosperity comes from faith and conviction that you and the universe are one. Look at the birds; they are not worried. They just fly. They know the wind will lift them up and carry them to their destination. That is what my life has been like for a long time. We must trust that the Divine will lift us up and carry us to our destination.

Many paths revere poverty as a path to the Divine. My teacher, Yogi Bhajan, always taught that prosperity opens the doorways to many things. If you revere poverty, you will probably remain impoverished. I've never been reluctant to make a lot of money. I've followed the guiding principles of prosperity throughout my life, and as a result, I've been able to use the abundance I have received to in turn give back in many ways. You have to have the conviction that if a lot of money comes to you, it would be in the best interest of the Universe. If you don't believe that, then you will sabotage anything that could bring you a lot of prosperity. You must know, at your core, that if prosperity comes to you, you will use it to serve.

Many people believe that money corrupts, and it can. But you don't need to believe it will corrupt you. The real art is generating success, and not being corrupt, having incredible integrity and becoming a great giver. You must continue to live by the guiding principles of prosperity, even when you achieve financial wealth, or you will soon lose it.

I don't think you need to have money to be happy. I think that happiness comes from being fully engaged in the flow of the Universe. When you are so engaged in the here and now, so fully present and focused on your daily work of doing and giving and receiving, that you are not worrying about the past or desiring things from the future, then prosperity can flow your way. That's why every sacred path tells you to sing God's praises. When you are singing with all 72 trillion cells, you are fully in the present and fully in the flow. The Universe can't help but take care of you.

Over the course of my life, I have learned through trial and error what opens me up to the flow of prosperity. In these pages, I have focused those things into ten unique principles to live by. These are the guiding principles of prosperity consciousness that I live by. Try them. You will see that abundance starts to flow your way.

GUIDING PRINCIPLE 1:

Have a Daily Practice to Strengthen the Self

I believe you need to nourish your soul on a daily basis. I believe that the soul is the core of all of one's being; it's the best part, the yolk in an egg, the highest self, the essence. The soul is where the most goodness is, the most light, the most kindness, the most compassion, and the more we bathe in that part of ourselves, the more we radiate the qualities that produce the most positive and magnificent life possible. You need to feel good about yourself to have a positive relationship with your soul.

One of the main reasons that you have a daily practice is to slowly build up your self-image. If your sense of self is low, it doesn't matter what you engage in, a high percentage of your thoughts will be accompanied by self-limiting beliefs. As you raise your self-image, it will be much easier for you to keep up and deal with adversity as it manifests.

When you get up in the morning, you need to start with a victory, whether it's taking a cold shower and then doing a strenuous yoga practice, or lacing up your sneakers and going for a run, or going to the gym and working out or taking a swim. You need to start the day with a victory. It builds momentum. Start with little victories and before you know it, big victories will manifest.

That's why the best time to do your daily practice is first thing in the morning, upon waking up, because it gives you this victorious feeling that carries over.

GUIDING PRINCIPLE 2:

Do Something that is True to Your Core

Do something that you have no duality about. Do something that every one of your 72 trillion cells believes is good for the entirety of existence. Then, it has to be good for you. Do something that you truly believe is in the best interest of your divine self and of the whole planet.

I've been doing sales training for years, and I can speak from my core to my students in a sales training class, but I can also pick up a guitar and be true to my core, or I can talk to my son and be true to my core as a parent. You bring your unique self to all your different roles in life. If you can feel that you are being true to your core in all aspects of your life, then you will find prosperity in every one of them.

There is a difference between being in love with a job and recognizing that you are doing something that is true to your core, something that is in harmony with your inner integrity. Whatever it is you are doing you need to be excelling at. I've always been a subscriber to the "s#*t or get off the pot" mentality. Don't hang around in a state of duality. You do not serve yourself or the people around you.

If you do not have conviction in what you are doing, then you've got to find something else, take the risk, and make the switch.

GUIDING PRINCIPLE 3:

Have Enough Conviction in the Self to Take Risks

You must believe in yourself, in your ability to recognize what is true to your core, and in the fact that what you choose to do is going to serve yourself and the Universe. Then, you must follow your true inner voice and understand what you are being called to do, and take that risk to do it!

When you know that you are doing something that is true to your core, there is no risk, because your choices are based on what is most important.

When you take a risk, you must be ready to handle the worst-case scenario. When I say "take a risk," you must ask yourself what is the worst thing that can happen? You might fail ... but then you take another risk and start something else. And eventually, if you are being true to your core, you are going to succeed.

Your actions are a manifestation of your beliefs. If you have conviction in yourself and you have conviction in your ability to succeed and be victorious, you will find a way to overcome every adversity.

GUIDING PRINCIPLE 4:

All Your Communications Must Radiate Good Will and Integrity

100% of your communications! 99% is not good enough, because if 1% of your communications are negative, it can wreak havoc on your universe. You can spend so much of your valuable time cleaning up the mess that the 1% created.

One ill-executed communication can take up so much of your valuable time. Have you ever said something to someone that maybe didn't come from the most positive space inside you, and then spent hours and hours and days and days cleaning up the mess?

Maintaining good will always serves you because your reputation precedes you. Additionally, if you do everything from a place of integrity, deep down you feel really, really good about yourself. Start fresh today living in integrity. I don't need to explain that. The word integrity just resonates.

There's an old expression that the hard way is the easy way and the easy way is the hard way. The easy way is to just get something done as long as you're feeling okay about it. But if you have not ensured good will all around, that ends up being much more difficult. It's worth taking on the extra work of ensuring everyone feels good.

Remember, good will and integrity must be constant and prosperity will follow.

What are you waiting for? At the end of that road is bliss.

GUIDING PRINCIPLE 5:

Master the Art of Win-Win Business

Master the art of win-win arrangements and develop the sensitivity that you're not really done until everybody walks away feeling good. You have to tune in to the other person and make sure they feel just as good as you.

You must learn to speak the language of win-win. You must always be searching for the balance point in all that you do. Every agreement you make must make all parties feel like they have won.

Sometimes you can inspire other people to agree to something that is not good for them. If people feel that they were a victim of your negotiating, there will be negative consequences. Look at the long-term consequences of everything. The long term eventually becomes the short term and eventually becomes the here and now.

Sometimes you feel like you're going to give more than you want to because you want to be done with something. It's a bad idea to walk away from the table feeling like you're a loser. You're paying a heavy toll. The resentment will build up. Your next interaction with that person will not be radiating the good will you're accustomed to.

What we are talking about here is developing the ability to see the consequence of the sequence. Remember that when everyone wins, you will have made a long-term ally. That is invaluable.

GUIDING PRINCIPLE 6:

An Attitude of Gratitude Brings Unlimited Abundance

Be a grateful person. Be grateful for this breath. Be grateful for all things and show that gratitude. Regularly express your gratitude. Everybody loves to work with grateful people. And when you express your gratitude, people want more gratitude, so they give you more.

I believe that gratitude is the most attractive quality of a human being. It is intoxicatingly attractive. Everyone wants to associate themselves with grateful people. All of my long-term relationships have endured because I continuously connect with the gratitude I have for those relationships. And I express it.

It might seem like a bit of an oxymoron because when you are grateful, you are not focused on what you can get. You just look around you and you are amazed by the abundance of your very existence, the miracle of each breath, the incredible people around you, the meal in front of you, and on and on. That child-like state of ecstatic gratitude is so attractive because it is contagious. It helps people remember when they were grateful and that maybe the cup is half full after all and not half empty.

When you show your gratitude to someone, they start to recognize what you have done for them, and a cycle of giving is born that will bring you great abundance.

GUIDING PRINCIPLE 7:

Trust Begets Trust

One of my foundational beliefs is that there is a very high probability that other people will live up to your trust in them. Many people don't trust themselves and haven't for a long time. As a result, everyone around them mistrusts them. When they are confronted by someone who offers them trust, especially by someone they respect and admire, they will knock themselves out to live up to that trust.

Instead of earning trust, you can command trust by trusting. It's a shortcut. If you are making people earn your trust, you are short-changing yourself. It takes too long. If you can help them reconnect with their core, it's beyond the conscious mind. It's happening on a level that is very deep, and it's a very beautiful thing.

So in a way, by believing in people, you make people believe in themselves. When I bring a person into one of my businesses, I say, "I already know you're going to do a magnificent job. I feel really good that you've agreed to come work with us, so thank you in advance."

And then, do you think there's a higher probability that they'll do a magnificent job if you approach it that way? It works! And you get a tenfold return. Look at how easy that was. And if they don't do a magnificent job, okay, so you have to re-inspire them—or maybe they prove they aren't the right person for that role, but why not start out by giving them and yourself the highest probability of success?

GUIDING PRINCIPLE 8:

Excel at What is in Front of You Today

Don't do anything in a halfhearted way. If you take a job, don't do it halfway. You never know what door will open up when you excel at whatever is in front of you.

If you take a look at any really successful person, I guarantee you they have strung together day after day after day of focusing on the success of that day. Having daily victories opens so many doors. When people see you excelling, they want to work with you in some way because excellence is contagious. It's viral.

Excelling is a habit you must learn. It's like a muscle that you develop, and doing a halfhearted job is the same thing. If you use the excuse that you aren't doing what you want to be doing, you overdevelop your mediocrity muscle. You get in the habit of doing things in a mediocre way, and then when you find something you really love, you are not programmed to excel.

For me, if I am working at something that doesn't feel like it's my ideal work situation, I chant. Chanting a mantra while working activates the positive mind. It's like a key. When my positive mind is turned on, I can only do things at a peak performance level.

People notice when you excel. When someone is constantly putting their full energy into something, you will always go back to that person. Excelling invites opportunity.

GUIDING PRINCIPLE 9:

Be Flexible and Learn How to Flow with Life

Be flexible on all levels: mental, physical and spiritual. When you meet obstacles, you know mentally, physically and spiritually, you can find your way around. It starts with the physical. Practice yoga! When you stretch your body, your mind is more expansive and things flow. You learn that there is a gentle way through all things.

In physics, when things are cold and tight, they break. When they are warm and flexible, they bend and sway under pressure. Learn to bend and sway with the pressures of life, find a way to work with the world around you, not try to stop it or change it.

When you are flexible, you are not stubborn. You see the whole creation as one entity. You see that everything is part of you, and you are part of everybody. Even in difficult situations, you recognize everybody as a teacher; some teachers teach you what to do and some teachers teach you what not to do.

You've got to be prepared for the unexpected; that's what the infinity is. In business and life, you can try to predict what's going to happen, but that's not always the way it works. You have to be able to bend and sway with whatever God delivers to your day. Expect the unexpected. Accept the unexpected. You are much less likely to get stuck if you are willing to be flexible and flow with life.

GUIDING PRINCIPLE 10:

When You Commit to Something, Do It!

Make sure that your word is your bond. Your commitment must be indelible. When you give your word to somebody, live up to it. You will have a reputation for integrity. When you know that you can stand by your word, it does wonders for your own self-image. Always do your best to honor your word. Bad news travels fast. In this day and age, when somebody doesn't honor a commitment, the word gets around.

When you make a commitment, be ready to stand by it. Everybody will want to work with you. Be as steady as the sun. Nobody wants to do business with a person who is up and down. No one will want to do business with you if they are not sure they can rely on you. Everyone wants a person who is consistent and whom they can count on. People want to know that even when there's a challenge, you will come through.

You must remember that people make their own commitments based on your commitments. If you break your word, you may be forcing someone else to break their word. This is the karmic cycle in immediate action. And when you don't stand by your commitments, you feel like you have to hide, and you feel like you are less than who you want to be. It destroys your self-image when you don't live up to your word.

Under-commit and over-deliver—it is a much better boat to be in.

These are the guiding principles of prosperity that I live by. I believe wholeheartedly that they will work for you in your life.

Try some of these meditations as well. They will help to build your prosperity consciousness. Use them as part of your daily practice. You will feel affirmed in your path.

I wish you great abundance, great prosperity and great happiness.

~ GuruGanesha Singh

Prosperity Affirmation:

Bountiful am I, Blissful am I,

Beautiful am I

Using the powerful tool of affirmation instills the strength of knowing your own abundance, joy and beauty. When you have the foundational strength in your sense of self, you can manifest your intentions into reality, and prosperity is yours.

Posture:

Sit in a comfortable position, one that will make you
feel completely able to focus on the affirmation you are reciting.
The hands are at rest.

Eyes:

Relax the eyes and close them.

Mantra:

Recite the words "Bountiful am I, Blissful am I, Beautiful am I" with the music. Feel these words permeate all 72 trillion cells of your being as you experience their truth. You are bountiful, you are blissful, you are beautiful. Know it! Experience it! Accept it!

You can do this for 1 minute, 3 minutes, 11 minutes or all day long. But commit to doing it consciously and consistently each day.

"The time has come for you to be you — a beautiful, bountiful, blissful human."

⫸ Yogi Bhajan (9/10/95)

Powerful Prosperity Meditation:

Har

There are a few mantras in Kundalini Yoga whose powerful results are so widely experienced that people revere them. This is one of those meditations. Everyone measures wealth and abundance differently. Many people have seen this meditation transform their careers, their finances, and their comfort level. It is a meditation that brings you the abundance and wealth that you truly need.

Yogi Bhajan talks about the power of this particular meditation:

"This meditation can be done for up to 11 minutes. It is so powerful in bringing prosperity that more than 11 minutes would be greedy."

"This meditation stimulates the mind, the moon center and Jupiter. When Jupiter and the moon come together, there is no way in the world you will not create wealth."

— Yogi Bhajan

FIGURE 2.1

FIGURE 2.2

Posture:

Sit in easy pose, with a light neck lock. Your spine is straight, your chest and sternum slightly lifted, your chin pulled slightly inward to allow the head and neck to stay straight and feeling slightly lifted.

(*NOTE:* Neck lock is called ***Jalandhar Bhand,*** which is said to help "untie the knot of Shiva." This "knot" or gateway is located at your brow point. When the energy of this knot is untied and flowing, you feel free of time and space. You associate yourself with the timelessness and non-duality of the soul and the Divine essence.)

Mudra:

Elbows are by the sides, forearms angled up and outward with the fingers at the level of the throat. The exercise begins with the palms facing down. Alternately hit the sides of the hands together. The Mercury (pinky) fingers and the Moon Mounds along the inner sides of the palm hit when the palms face up (Figure 2.1). When the palms are facing down, the sides of the Jupiter (index) fingers touch, and the thumbs cross below the hands, with the right thumb under the left (Figure 2.2). Yogi Bhajan said that the thumbs crossing this way is the key to the meditation.

Eyes:

Relax the eyelids and allow them to hang 9/10ths closed. Feel the eyes gently pull together to look through the veil of the eyelashes at the tip of the nose. You will feel the eye muscles stretch, creating a gentle pressure along the inner side of the eyes. This is an important part of the meditation, so try to maintain the eye position.

Mantra: Har

Chant continuously from the navel, using the tip of the tongue. Chant with strength.

Time:

Continue for 3-11 minutes.

End:

Inhale deeply, hold the breath, exhale. Repeat 2 times and relax.

Nanak's Abundant Gifts Meditation for Financial Prosperity: Bahota Karam

"Prosperity is a state produced immediately by the mind. When the sun comes out of the clouds, everything is lit. When the mind comes out of duality, prosperity is there. And the 25th Pauri has the power to take away duality..."

— *Yogi Bhajan*

To be prosperous, you must eliminate duality. You must live in certainty. Know that you are one with all of creation; you are a part of the greater consciousness of the Universe around you. Remember that wealth and abundance are part of a flow of energy. If you realize that nothing separates you from that which is around you, you open yourself up to being within the flow, and abundance can flow to you. Have no duality about it.

The 25th Pauri of Japji, written by the first Guru of the Sikhs, Guru Nanak, is an incredible rhapsody of joy and bliss written by a fully enlightened being. Nanak sings of the abundant gifts of God. Reciting the 25th Pauri 11 times within a day, Yogi Bhajan taught, would elevate you into a space of tremendous achievement. Clearing the grey clouds from your consciousness brings out the shining sun, and with it comes a pot of gold at the end of the rainbow!

Posture:

Sit in easy pose, with a straight spine. The hands are either in the lap or resting on the knees in gyan mudra (first fingers and thumb tips are touching).

Mantra:

Bahotaa karam likhiaa na jaa-ay.
Vadaa dataa til na tamaay.
Kaytay mange jodh apaar.
Kaythaa ganat nahee veechaar.
Kaytay khap tuteh vikar.
Kaytay lai lai mukar paa-eh.
Kaytay moorakh khaahee khaa-eh.
Kaytiaa dookh bhookh sad maar.
Ay-eh bhe daat tayree daataar

Band khaalasee bhanai hoe.
Hor aakh na sakai koe.
Jay ko khaa-ik akhaan paae.
Oh jaanai jaytee-aa muh khaa-ay.
Aapay jaanay aapay day-eh.
Aakheh se bhe kay-ee kay-eh.
Jis no bakhsay siphat saalaah.
Naanak paatisaahee paatisaah.

Translation:

There is so much karma , it isn't possible to write about it all.
The Great Giver does not hold anything back,
not even the smallest sesame seed.
Many warriors beg to merge with You.
Many count your ways, but never truly see You.
Many are exhausted, having wrecked themselves in their vices.
Many take all your gifts and deny that they have them.
Many fools sit idly and fill themselves with food.
Many are surrounded by need and pain and hunger.
But even these things are gifts from You, Great Giver.
Enslavement and freedom are both gifts from you.
There is nothing more to be said.
Speaking only to hear the sound of one's voice fills one with shame.
You alone know. You alone give.
Blessed are the few who can speak of it truthfully.
Blessed are they who can sing of Your true gifts.
Nanak, these are the Royalty of Royalty.

"If you recite the 25th Pauri [Japji] eleven times a day, it will bring you prosperity and wealth. It is a promise. There are many people who have done it and they became prosperous."

"The 25th Pauri adds up to seven. It is a platform of levitation. It means wherever you are and whatever you are, this pauri will elevate you, levitate you, to the point of achievement, no matter what!"

Yogi Bhajan

Meditation for Your Life's Needs:

Ardas Bhaee

This is the mantra for answered prayers. Sometimes, you don't even know what it is you need that will answer your prayers. Just let go of what you think you want or need. This meditation will bring you what you truly need. You will connect directly with your soul and open yourself to an experience of peace and prosperity.

Guru Amar Das is the third of the Sikh Gurus. His life and teachings embodied generosity, kindness and a strong sense that all people are to be treated equal. Guru Ram Das, his son-in-law, is the fourth of the Sikh Gurus. His life and teachings embodied deep humility, abiding gratitude and selfless service.

Ram means **God's servant**. When you send a prayer to Guru Ram Das, it is his duty to bring it to God. So lay your life's needs in the lap of Guru Ram Das, and let God send them your way.

"Normally there is no power in the human but the power of prayer. And to do prayer, you have to put your mind and body together and then pray from the soul. Ardas Bhaee is a mantra prayer. If you sing it, your mind, body and soul automatically combine and without saying what you want, the need of the life is adjusted. That is the beauty of this prayer."

— *Yogi Bhajan*

FIGURE 4

Posture:

Sit in easy pose with a straight spine. Relax the upper arms by the sides and bring the hands up to the level of the heart. Interlace the fingers and the grip tighter than normal. (Figure 4)

Eyes:

Relax the eyelids and allow them to hang
9/10ths closed. Feel the eyes gently pull together
to look through the veil of the eyelashes at the
tip of the nose. You will feel the eye muscles
stretch, creating a gentle pressure along the inner
side of the eyes. This is an important part of the
meditation, so try to maintain the eye position.

Time:

Continue for 3-11 minutes.

End:

Inhale, hold briefly, exhale and relax.

Complete Mantra:

Ardas Bhaee, Amar Das Guru,
Amar Das Guru, Ardas Bhaee,
Ram Das Guru, Ram Das Guru,
Ram Das Guru, Sachee Sahee.

Translation:

The prayer has been given to
Guru Amar Das. The prayer is
manifested by Guru Ram Das.
The miracle is complete.

Fearless Prosperity Meditation:
Har Har Har Har Gobinday

This mantra, given by Yogi Bhajan, contains Guru Gobind Singh's prayer to bring courage and fearlessness into your life. This is a powerful mantra, a warrior mantra. It will help you have the strength to see the obstacles before you and the consciousness to find your way around them, over them and through them.

This meditation connects your personal journey to fearlessness with the global and collective consciousness of the Infinite. As you find your own strength and courage, you are lifted 10 times higher than yourself through your connection with the Universal strength and courage that surrounds you. Soak it in and expand into it.

Prosperity is yours when you know you are capable of achieving it. Use this meditation to give you that strength of will to forge ahead.

"Meditation is a foundation of human prosperity to live healthy, happy and holy. It's a key to successful creative life."

Yogi Bhajan

Posture:

Sit in easy pose, with a light Jalandhar Bandh.

Mudra:

Press the thumb and ring (4th) finger together. Chant in rhythm with the music. Pull in the navel point with each repetition of Har. Chant for 11, 31, or 62 minutes. (Figure 5)

FIGURE 5

Eyes:

Relax the eyelids and allow them to hang 9/10ths closed. Feel the eyes gently pull together to look through the veil of the eyelashes at the tip of the nose. You will feel the eye muscles stretch, creating a gentle pressure along the inner side of the eyes. This is an important part of the meditation, so try to maintain the eye position

Har Har Har Har Gobinday
Har Har Har Har Mukhunday
Har Har Har Har Udharay
Har Har Har Har Aparay
Har Har Har Har Hariang
Har Har Har Har Kariang
Har Har Har Har Nirnamay
Har Har Har Har Akamay

This mantra contains the 8 facets of God:
Gobinday, the One who sustains us
Mukhunday, the One who liberates us
Udharay, the One who uplifts us
Aparay, the One who is Infinite
Hariang, the One who does everything
Kariang, the One for whom grace is done
Nirnamay, the One who is nameless and desireless
Akamay, the One who is all by itself

Har is a "Shakti Yog (power) Mantra." Har is the creative energy of
God. The four repetitions of Har give power to all aspects and provide
the power to break down barriers of the past.

Gurprasad Meditation: Guru's Nectar

This is a meditation that teaches you to accept the gifts of prosperity.

Posture:

Sit in easy pose with a straight spine. Cup the hands together in front of the heart as though you are waiting for water to be poured into your hands. Press the arms against the rib cage. (Figure 6)

FIGURE 6

Eyes:

Relax the eyelids and allow them to hang 9/10ths closed. Feel the eyes gently pull together to look through the veil of the eyelashes at the tip of the nose. You will feel the eye muscles stretch, creating a gentle pressure along the inner side of the eyes. As the meditation progresses, allow the eyes to close if they begin to feel heavy.

Time:

You can do this meditation for any length of time. Try starting with 3 minutes and building up to 11 minutes.

Feel that you are receiving the sweetest nectar into the cupped vessel of your hands. Feel the collective energy of the Universe pouring its abundance into your hands. Know that you deserve to receive the gift of this nectar. This posture is a posture of receiving, and you must surrender to the will of the Great Giver and know that you deserve to have prosperity. Know that your cup truly "runneth over."

Suggestions While Practicing:

❋

KUNDALINI YOGA AS TAUGHT *by* YOGI BHAJAN

COVERING THE HEAD: Covering the head helps one become aware of and control the subtle energies in the body. It enables you to command your sixth center, the Ajna Chakra. It stabilizes the cerebral matter and the 26 parts of the brain, which are interlocked with the neurological system and electromagnetic field. Covering the head creates a focus of the functional circuit of the hemispheres of the brain and tunes the neurological system. It is generally recommended to cover the head while practicing Kundalini Yoga.

ADI MANTRA: Before practicing these meditations, it is suggested that you first "tune in." Yogi Bhajan gave the Adi Mantra for this purpose.

ONG NAMO GURU DEV NAMO
Translation: I bow to the Creative Wisdom, I bow to the Divine Teacher within.

This mantra is used for "tuning in" to the divine flow and self-knowledge within each of us as well as linking us to Yogi Bhajan and the Golden Chain of teachers. It is chanted three times at the start of any Kundalini Yoga practice.

Bibliography & Resources:

BOOKS:

The Aquarian Teacher Textbook, Level 1, by Yogi Bhajan, Ph.D., published by Kundalini Research Institute

Japji Sahib by Guru Nanak – a daily prayer from the Siri Guru Granth Sahib, the sacred Sikh scriptures

Self Experience, by Harijot Kaur Khalsa, published by Kundalini Research Institute

Yoga for Prosperity, by Siri Kirpal Kaur, published by Yogi Ji Press

MUSIC:

Bountiful am I, Blissful am I, Beautiful am I by GuruGanesha Singh and Snatam Kaur
~ adapted from the album *Pure Ganesh*

Prosperity Har by Prabhu Nam Kaur and Snatam Kaur
~ adapted from the album *Seasons of the Soul*

Bahota Karam by Sat Hari Singh and Hari Bhajan Kaur
~ adapted from the album *Servant of the Heart*

Ardas Bhaee by Mirabai Ceiba
~ from the album *Ocean*

Har Har Har Har Gobinday by GuruGanesha Singh
~ adapted from the album *Kundalini Surjhee*

Visit www.SpiritVoyage.com/kundalinitoolkits for more information and resources